Self-Esteem

Gain An Understanding Of The Psychology Of Women
And Employ Incremental Measures To Alleviate
Instances Of Diminished Self-Esteem Through The
Utilization Of Affirmative Statements And Embracing
Self-Acceptance

Rod Beauchemin

TABLE OF CONTENT

The Ugly Truth 1

Understanding Self-Esteem 23

The True Empowerment Of Self-Assurance 28

Confidence – Observation 48

Introversion And Its Impact On Interpersonal Relationships 56

Understanding Body Language 78

The Rationale Behind Establishing Objectives 98

Developing Self-Love 104

Joy And Self-Recognition Function In Tandem. 113

The Efficacy Of Optimistic Mindset 127

The Ugly Truth

A mere fraction of individuals, precisely 0.1%, actually apply guidance or enroll in educational programs; diligently navigating from one course to another devoid of purpose or direction. Should you aspire to belong to that exceptional percentile, which not only embraces but achieves success, I urge you to accompany me for a brief 15 minutes. I possess unwavering certainty that this interaction will significantly aid you in your journey.

As previously mentioned, a vast majority of individuals, approximately 99.99%, experience failure due to their failure to take initiative and initiate action. Merely assimilating information will not lead to successful outcomes. It is imperative that you take action in response to it.

Now it's your turn...

Statistically speaking, approximately 99.99% of readers do not progress beyond this point. Therefore, your presence here indicates that you possess an exceptional mindset and are committed to initiating transformative actions.

WHAT IS THIS METHOD?

There is no longer a need to wait any further... allow me to impart my insights to you. Now...

Studies indicate that a significant portion of the American population, and potentially individuals worldwide, possesses diminished self-esteem. To put it differently, a considerable majority of individuals face challenges related to their self-perception. It is not uncommon for me to remark, metaphorically, that among a group of three individuals, only one is likely to possess a healthy level of self-esteem, highlighting the scarcity of individuals with positive self-worth.

When your self-esteem and self-confidence are diminished, it may result in the acceptance of unsatisfying and potentially harmful relationships, the avoidance of necessary risks to attain your aspirations, and the inclination to conform to less than what you merit in life.

Therefore, within the contents of this book, I aim to impart a selection of approaches by which one may enhance their self-esteem and cultivate their self-assurance.

To begin with, allow me to inform you that there was a time when my self-esteem was not always present. Due to my father's perfectionist tendencies, I was frequently plagued by feelings of inadequacy and a persistent belief that I fell short of expectations.

Nevertheless, after dedicating significant time and effort to personal growth endeavors and participating in numerous educational sessions, I managed to cultivate a considerable level of self-esteem. I came to realize that the root of my perceived inadequacy lay not in my actual capabilities, but rather in the negative thoughts and beliefs I held about myself.

Subsequent to my acquisition of knowledge, it has come to my attention that the veracity lies in the fact that nearly all of us harbor an underlying conviction that we possess deficiencies in one form or another. You may easily complete the empty space and determine which option suits you best:

- I lack the necessary intellectual capacity • I do not possess sufficient cognitive abilities • My level of intelligence falls short in this regard
- I do not possess sufficient physical attractiveness

- I do not possess sufficient athleticism. • My level of physical fitness does not meet the requirements. • I lack the necessary athletic prowess. • My abilities in sports are not up to par.
- My communication skills are lacking • I am unable to express myself effectively • I struggle to communicate my thoughts clearly
- I do not possess the qualities that make me deserving of love • I lack the necessary attributes to be deemed lovable or deserving of love • I perceive myself as unworthy of love or lacking in love-worthy characteristics
- I lack the necessary competence, financial resources, skills, talent, and sense of humor, among other things.

To put it succinctly, I lack the adequacy to be considered "blank," allowing ample room for individuals to conceptualize their own interpretation of this blank, as we all possess a unique quality to contribute in filling it.

According to Dr. Nathaniel Brennan, a distinguished figure in the field of self-esteem development, it is argued that a person's elevated level of self-esteem emanates from a deep-seated sense of being affable, skilled, and noteworthy.

Presently, affectionate pertains to the subjective assessment of one's inherent value and capacity to be loved. Competent, on the other hand, signifies the conviction in one's ability to effectively navigate unforeseen circumstances, achieve desired outcomes, and effectively address any obstacles or adversities encountered along the way.

Presently, it is of great importance that one perceives that their existence holds significance. Specifically, it pertains to the notion that one's identity and actions hold substantial value, contributing to the betterment of others' lives.

Now, let us examine several methods by which we can enhance our sense of being worthy, competent, and prominent, thereby bolstering one's self-esteem.

Presently, this subject matter possesses the potential to be further expounded upon as a comprehensive three-day seminar, given the copious amount of approaches available. However, for the purposes of brevity, allow us to concentrate solely on a select few fundamental principles that I aim to convey through this written work, which you can readily implement as of today.

Initially, let us examine methods for augmenting your sense of desirability. Now, in order to maximize your likability factor, it is essential to embrace the notion that every aspect of your being is flawlessly magnificent as it stands.

This does not imply that you are incapable of personal growth and development. Rather, it suggests that you are content with your present state and that it is acceptable to express all of your emotions without reservation.

It is permissible to experience feelings of anger, fear, sorrow, confusion, uncertainty, desire for more, fatigue, and being overwhelmed, and to also feel a sense of pride, enthusiasm, hope, excitement, joy, happiness, appreciation, and the complete spectrum of human emotions.

Now, undoubtedly, you can acquire the knowledge and skills necessary to prevent the continual generation of suffering, sorrow and resentment in your life, but it is imperative that you acknowledge and embrace your current circumstances.

Currently, women have the capability to experience anger and men have the capacity to develop the ability to express their emotions through tears. Numerous individuals have been indoctrinated to eschew such behavior through societal messaging that emphasizes the importance of feminine refinement for women and discourages men from exhibiting weakness.

And when we accept that we shut parts of ourselves down as unacceptable.

I extend an invitation to you to courageously express something of great significance to you that you have hesitated to disclose to someone over the course of this week.

I was acquainted with an individual who resided in Argentina. He is an individual who exhibits a profound dedication to personal development, and achieves great success in various aspects of his life. However, he harbored significant dissatisfaction within his relationship, which he struggled to acknowledge within himself and articulate to others. He experienced a sense of moral responsibility and internal conflict if he were to separate from his spouse.

Hence, he sought assistance and was essentially advised to recognize the inefficacy of his current approach.

He was compelled to acknowledge his disbelief in the feasibility of the endeavor and the initial step he had to take was to contact a legal professional and initiate the proceedings.

He exhibited profound discomfort in response to the situation; nevertheless, he proceeded to carry out the task. Subsequently, he expressed that he experienced a marked reduction in weightiness. He experienced an amplified sense of liberation, as if he possessed the ability to fashion the desired trajectory of his life.

Therefore, the initial step is to recognize and openly acknowledge any emotions you may be experiencing, subsequently committing yourself to the process of effectively expressing those feelings and taking the necessary actions that result from doing so.

Another viable approach to enhance your likability quotient is to proactively engage and integrate yourself into the social spheres of others. I understand that the current circumstances of widespread lockdown pose challenges, as I write this book. However, with the aid of modern tools such as cell phones and communication platforms like Facetime, Skype, Zoom, and others, it is possible to connect with friends, family members, and online support communities, enabling one to actively participate.

Embrace your true self and find solace in the assurance that you are cherished precisely as you are. Now, my spouse serves as a prime illustration of this concept.

She engages in regular teleconferences with her sisters and one of her nieces on a weekly basis, maintains frequent communication with her best friend through multiple telephone conversations in a week, conducts monthly discussions with her brother, participates in monthly conferencing sessions with two women's support groups she is a member of, and partakes in a scheduled weekly family facetime call involving both her and me.

Consequently, she experiences a profound sense of inclusion, affection, and self-worth. Moreover, she recently confided in me that she courageously disclosed her dissatisfaction with the direction of a support group she had been attending for more than a year.

It transpires that a number of individuals shared similar sentiments, albeit choosing not to voice their thoughts, and collectively decided to modify the group's structure. Her candid expression of her genuine emotions played a vital role in fostering the development of the group.

Furthermore, an alternate approach to developing a sense of being deserving of love is to allocate sufficient time to cultivate self-love and self-care. This may encompass engaging in activities that promote personal well-being, such as indulging in a leisurely bath accompanied by melodic tunes, practicing meditation, dedicating an afternoon to immersing oneself in a thought-provoking novel by a preferred writer, attending to personal grooming, requesting a nurturing massage from a partner, or arranging for a cooked meal prepared on one's behalf.

Rising from one's workstation and embarking on a leisurely stroll, be it a brief jaunt or an extended amble, participating in yoga routines, engaging in cherished pastimes, or simply basking in the warmth of the sun whilst idling away the time.

Take time to do what you want. It truly plays a pivotal role in fostering self-care.

Now, let us explore the realm of confidence. One of the exercises I employ during meetings entails inviting each participant to compile a comprehensive list of 100 accomplishments they have achieved in their lifetime.

Additionally, these accomplishments include completing middle school, completing high school, acquiring the skill of driving and obtaining a driver's license, securing my initial employment, successfully relocating from Indiana to California, gaining acceptance into the fraternity or sorority of my preference during college, acquiring proficiency in the German language, nurturing and raising two commendable children, overcoming the habit of smoking, achieving a weight loss of 25 pounds, settling my bank loan, entering into matrimony, extricating myself from an abusive relationship, acquiring culinary skills, among others.

We have all experienced numerous achievements, although we often overlook them and have a tendency to measure our successes against those of prominent individuals such as Bill Gates, Tom Hanks, Michelle Obama, Taylor Swift, or Michael Jordan. It is worth noting that drawing comparisons can lead to feelings of discontentment, as I often remark that such comparisons pave the way to unhappiness.

Now, in addition, there are two additional strategies that can be employed to cultivate self-esteem, namely maintaining a record of accomplishments and engaging in the mirror exercise. Both of these strategies center around recognizing and affirming your achievements.

A triumph register is essentially a formal documentation tool, such as a notebook or journal, dedicated to capturing each and every accomplishment, be it momentous or minor, accomplished throughout the course of the day.

You engage in this activity on a daily basis. These achievements need not be monumental; they can consist of tasks such as waking up promptly, arriving punctually at work, consuming a nutritious breakfast, resisting the temptation of a chocolate cake, engaging in treadmill exercises or a 30-minute Pilates session, practicing meditation, repeating affirmations and visualization exercises, contacting five potential clients, conducting a highly effective coaching session with Alice, enjoying meaningful moments with my children, dedicating 20 minutes to enhancing my social media visibility through educational literature, successfully executing my inaugural Facebook live session, and so forth. You get the idea.

The mirror exercise entails positioning oneself in front of a sizable mirror prior to retiring for the night, and engaging in a disciplined, self-assuring dialogue with one's own reflection. By gazing intensely into the reflection of my own eyes, I initiate the process by uttering my name, "Alvaro," consequently summoning forth my essence. "Subsequently, you

acknowledge and commend yourself for your accomplishments in three distinct domains:
Attainments, achievements, endeavors undertaken, and tasks successfully accomplished.
Furthermore, you maintained various disciplines such as physical exercise, engaging in workouts, carrying out stretching routines, dedicating time to meditation, partaking in gratitude exercises, visualizing your aspirations, ensuring adequate vitamin intake, staying hydrated, engaging in social media posting or indulging in inspirational literature.

In conclusion, any instances in which you exhibited self-control, such as refraining from consuming a third glass of wine, opting out of indulging in a sugary dessert, maintaining a balanced sleep schedule instead of succumbing to late-night binge-watching, avoiding conflicts with your partner, or limiting excessive engagement with video games.

Finally, the discourse culminates with the direct expression of affection, namely, the utterance of the phrase "I love you".

You recite the statement silently and maintain steady eye contact with yourself, allowing the words to resonate within your being.

Having a sense of significance, wherein one feels that their personal worth and the impact they make on others are important, can be enhanced through actively engaging in actions that bring about positive changes in the lives of others.

You could consider dedicating a few hours per week to engage in volunteer activities. You have the opportunity to offer your services as a volunteer at a nearby food bank. I have recently come across an account wherein an individual became aware of the act of farmers discarding their surplus crops due to overproduction. Demonstrating resourcefulness, this individual devised a method to procure said food and contribute it to nearby food banks, thus catering to the needs of the homeless and unemployed individuals.

Single parents who are employed require childcare services, individuals who feel isolated are in need of companionship, those who have experienced the loss of a loved one require grief counseling, and there exist entrepreneurs facing difficulties who could benefit from your expertise in coaching and business guidance.

Even the act of providing financial support to local and global organizations engaged in the rescue and rehabilitation of animals, the support and sheltering of refugees, the pursuit of social equity, or the promotion of environmental sustainability, can imbue one with an enhanced perception of personal impact, instilling a profound sense of significance and direction.

Therefore, endeavor to enact positive change in the lives of others. And now, here is an additional uncomplicated suggestion: disengage from the association of subpar circumstances.

In essence, what I am implying is to create a comprehensive inventory encompassing all individuals with whom you engage, be it in physical encounters or through virtual means. Subsequently, I advise you to introspectively evaluate each person's influence upon your well-being, discerning whether they offer encouragement and support or conversely, exhibit detrimental tendencies. Do they ignite inspiration within me or do they extinguish my enthusiasm.

Do I experience an enhanced sense of self-worth following my interactions with them, or does my self-esteem diminish?

Subsequently, sever connections with individuals who have a detrimental influence on you, such as those who incessantly complain, whine, make excuses, engage in negative gossip, or display pessimism. These individuals are characterized by their overall negativity.

Choose to associate with individuals who exude positivity, uplift your spirits, have unwavering belief in your potential, provide unwavering support, offer genuine encouragement, and genuinely desire your ultimate well-being.

If you are unable to locate them within your immediate social circle comprising of friends and family, consider searching for them through online platforms such as Youtube, Facebook, and Instagram. Consume TED Talks or motivational videos, and similar sources of inspiration. There is an extensive array of video podcasts and complimentary online courses available, amounting to thousands of hours, that can serve to elevate your knowledge and nourish your mind.

As an illustration, one could easily input the query "top 100 motivational podcasts" into the search bar, which will yield a selection of commendable options.

I have a close acquaintance who dedicates a substantial portion of her daily routine to engaging in a two-hour listening activity, resulting in her current state as one of the most contented and efficient individuals I have had the pleasure of knowing.

This alternative is far superior to dedicating two hours to consuming unsettling news on television.

Additionally, I would like to present a few additional expeditious methods that one can employ.

Understanding Self-Esteem

One may gain a better comprehension of self-esteem by examining the attributes of individuals who possess a deficiency or absence of self-esteem. There are three classifications into which men with low self-esteem can be categorized:

The Withdrawn Guy
The Purist
Mister Grin

The Withdrawn Guy

This is the most widely acknowledged category of an individual with diminished self-worth. He is frequently aligned with negativity in his thoughts and behaviors. He perceives himself to be lacking in ability and competence, thereby positioning himself as a disadvantaged or underperforming individual. His behavior is frequently guided by a sense of pessimism regarding both his capabilities and his character, leading him to frequently utter statements such as "I am unable to," "I should not," "I was incapable," and "I am left with no alternative." When faced with a challenging predicament, his initial response is to escape or avoid. He lacks sufficient self-confidence to persevere in any demanding circumstances. Frequently, his thoughts are inundated with a multitude of hypothetical inquiries, causing him to recoil in trepidation towards the unfamiliar.

The Purist

This particular individual frequently displays attributes indicative of high self-assurance: unwavering in their convictions, consistently assuming leadership roles, and effectively managing any given circumstance. The distinguishing factor between him and a truly confident individual lies in the alternate facet of his character. The purist frequently exhibits a demeanor characterized by seriousness, meticulousness, anxiety, and tension. He leverages his position of authority to conceal his inherent lack of self-confidence. He encounters difficulty in placing trust in others and will solely assign tasks as a means to assert his authority. When circumstances become disorderly, he tends to attribute failure to others. His self-perception is characterized by such elevated regard that he remains impervious to criticism, suggestions, or instructions. An individual exhibiting this inherent inclination possesses a narrow perspective on the world. He refrains from embarking on new experiences due to the fear of his vulnerabilities becoming exposed. He adheres strictly to prescribed procedures and views innovation with disapproval.

Mister Grin

Initially, you may perceive this individual as humorous and amiable, fostering a sense of compatibility. Frequently, he presents himself as joyful and he derives pleasure from capturing the focus of others through his clever comments. He thoroughly enjoys engaging in playful pranks and consistently displays a willingness to participate in audacious challenges. He establishes a correlation between his self-perceived value and thoughtless displays of boldness, masculinity, and assertions of his masculine identity. In actuality, he maintains a cheerful facade in order to conceal his inner vulnerabilities. Over time, his jovial demeanor becomes increasingly grating to others due to his offensive comments that straddle the line of racism, sexism, or any expression that promotes a sense of superiority over others. It is unsurprising that his utmost apprehension revolves around fostering a committed romantic partnership, given his inability to regard himself with the desired level of earnestness.

What factors give rise to these particular dispositions? What factors have led to the manifestation of such characteristics in men?

The True Empowerment Of Self-Assurance

Allow me to impart to you a confidential piece of information. This information is classified due to the reluctance of many individuals to acknowledge it. The truth is that a substantial number of individuals exhibit uncertainties and a deficiency of self-assurance. Now, please refrain from becoming overly enthusiastic. The absence of firm belief does not necessarily entail a complete absence of self-assurance. They lack enough confidence. To put it differently, it falls beneath the standard necessary for them to function at their optimal level in daily activities.

Now, this revelation is readily evident. One can simply observe the lives of individuals they are acquainted with, and it is highly probable that 80% of the instances will showcase an existence not fully attaining its utmost capacity. Stated differently, they possess significant untapped potential, yet they choose to lead a life that falls considerably short of realizing this potential. They are providing payment; consequently, they are assuming a subordinate position. They are not fully embracing the opportunities that life has to offer within their capabilities.

Once more, this is attributed to their deficiency in self-assurance. They do not possess a sufficient level of confidence. Hence, individuals who exhibit an elevated degree of self-assurance possess an inherent magnetism. Individuals who possess a deficiency in self-assurance tend to be attracted to individuals who exhibit unwavering certainty. Now, refrain from becoming overly enthused. It is readily apparent to discern the favorable aspect of this situation; it is effortless to observe individuals who are attracted to your presence, thereby providing reinforcement and motivation. The underlying fact, even if left unsaid, is that I am drawn to you due to your possession of an attribute that I lack to a significant degree.

Nonetheless, one can also inadvertently attract individuals in an unfavorable manner. Certain individuals may experience a deficit in their self-assurance, which they are acutely aware of, prompting them to target individuals who possess an innate sense of confidence, aiming to undermine, reveal vulnerabilities, or subject them to uncomfortable situations. There consistently exists that degree of variation.

Ultimately, it can be determined that individuals who portray confidence, irrespective of the manner in which they do so, possess an inherent ability to captivate others due to their ability to induce a sense of ease and comfort within their vicinity. Furthermore, a state of adverse magnetism arises due to the potential envy that individuals may harbor towards your possessions or achievements. They desire comfort, yet they are under the impression that they must assail you in order to compensate for their own insecurities.

Nevertheless, when one possesses self-assurance, they inherently exude a captivating aura. Indeed, individuals often meet the expectations and desires of others with regard to providing them comfort and support. To put it differently, those in your vicinity are seeking someone to provide them with guidance and direction. They resemble disoriented sheep in search of a guiding shepherd. I understand that this statement may come across as offensive, as openly criticizing someone and comparing them to a sheep could potentially lead to physical confrontations.

However, it must be acknowledged that individuals, to varying degrees, possess a deficiency in self-assurance, and they are cognizant of this fact. This is the reason why they instinctively are drawn to individuals who possess a commendable degree of easily observable and readily discernible self-assurance. Why does this happen? What is the reason behind individuals' pursuit of effective leadership? Indeed, individuals who exude confidence have a remarkable ability to instill a sense of possibility in those in their presence. This exemplifies the characteristics of effective leadership. When one stimulates the belief in the feasibility of certain things among those in one's vicinity, an insatiable fascination and admiration is evoked. Why? Given autonomy or placed in an independent situation, they perceive matters to be more challenging than they actually are. They hold the belief that circumstances are not conducive to easiness and that various impediments exist throughout the journey.

When you make your presence felt and ignite inspiration within them, leading them to believe in the realm of possibilities, they cannot resist but be compelled to take notice. You compel them to engage in thought processes beyond their usual capacity. If one spends a substantial amount of time in the company of self-assured individuals, they have a remarkable ability to instill in others the belief that not only are things achievable, but highly likely to occur. This is the quality that individuals seek in effective leadership. This is the desired social dynamic sought after by individuals.

Have you ever observed collectives of adolescents and discerned varying degrees of assertiveness among them? Surprisingly, the introduction of an influential leader of a similar age can inspire and propel a previously timid group of adolescent boys to engage in various activities, yielding unexpected outcomes. Certainly, this scenario can yield either advantageous or disadvantageous outcomes.

Many instances of hooligan violence and gang violence reported in the media often revolve around groups of adolescents who are influenced by one or two leaders, thereby fostering the belief that certain actions are not only feasible but likely to occur. Engaging in the act of pilfering from an establishment that retails alcoholic beverages? If the leader is absent from the equation, then that idea becomes purely speculative. Once a suitable individual is introduced to the group, it is merely a question of time until they collectively commit the act of robbing a liquor establishment.

Do you perceive the operational mechanics of this? This has the potential to result in either a positive or negative outcome. However, it is undeniably true that individuals who exude confidence possess the ability to instill in those around them a sense that not only are things possible, but they are highly probable. I cannot attest to your perspective, but in my opinion, that unequivocally epitomizes the concept of power.

Know your self-worth

Comprehending one's self-worth is unrelated to scrutinizing one's financial status; it pertains to...

You, as a person you embody in your daily existence. We extend consideration, affection, and contemplation towards others

How often do we meet the requirements that are expected of us? Your self-esteem is contingent upon

The level of self-assurance you possess directly influences your true sense of self-worth.

A strong sense of self-assurance fosters independence, contentment, flexibility, and the ability to readily adapt.

to adapt, collaborative action, and a positive perspective towards any situation. Undesirable or low

Excessive self-assurance often gives rise to irrational thoughts, melancholy, and fear of the unknown.

novelty, rigidity, proactiveness, and a pessimistic perspective overall.

Our perception of ourselves significantly influences the perception others have of us, should we be

When we are exuberant, wearing a broad smile, and emanating a sense of unwavering assurance, others perceive us as individuals whom they desire to have in their company.

In the event that we hold ourselves in high regard and portray our proximity, others would likewise perceive it.

You will also be regarded, as how can one expect to receive respect from others if they themselves do not show respect.

don't regard yourself? Thus, the cultivation and development of self-esteem correspond intricately with the cultivation and development of one's confidence.

High self esteem

If you possess a strong sense of self-assurance, you are likely to recognize specific attributes in yourself.

In terms of self-perception, qualities associated with a strong sense of assurance or self-assurance are

• You possess a steadfast sense of self and exhibit unwavering confidence in your abilities

- By doing so, you afford yourself the opportunity to express your true emotions to others

- You do not experience any difficulty in forming close relationships with others.

- One can acquire self-awareness and take pride in one's achievements.

throughout everyday life

- You are poised to absolve both yourself and others for mistakes.

Low self esteem

Likewise, if you experience difficulties with self-worth or diminished self-assurance, then

You are advised to explore a particular instance in your deliberations and approaches, in the event that you

If one encounters challenges related to low self-assurance, they may observe the following characteristics within themselves.

- Self-assurance is essential for you, yet your reliability is remarkably inconsistent.

- You have difficulties with establishing and sustaining emotional intimacy in a romantic relationship.

- Your true emotions never become evident • You consistently conceal your genuine feelings • Your actual sentiments are always hidden

- You consistently fail to recognize and take credit for your accomplishments.

- You possess the inability to provide excuses for yourself or others

- You consistently resist change in every opportunity • You consistently show opposition towards change in every given opportunity • You consistently express resistance towards change at every chance

Developing your self-worth

There are numerous methodologies through which one can enhance their self-esteem and transition into a proficient individual.

To foster a strongly optimistic and nourishing perspective towards oneself, here are a few suggestions for formulating and

boosting your self-esteem.

- Instead of acknowledging the analysis of various demographics, it is advisable to listen attentively to their perspectives.
- Avoid dismissing the analysis of diverse groups and instead focus on actively listening to their perspectives.

expressing and deriving benefits from it.

- Allocate regular intervals of time to dedicate to self-reflection, introspection, and developing a comprehensive understanding of your thoughts and emotions.

Consider the credibility of your assertions and imagine transforming your unfavorable ones into increasingly constructive ones.

- Commemorate and take pride in even the most minor achievements that you have accomplished.

Engage in a consistent activity that brings you joy, such as taking a leisurely walk during daylight hours or

experiencing a sudden and intense burst of air pockets in a shower-like manner.

- It is advisable to refrain from depriving oneself of something one values, once one becomes cognizant of its significance.

One should abstain from engaging in such behavior; if one does, it is advisable to cease dwelling on it and refrain from self-blame.

- Engage in a purposeful and deliberate internal dialogue, repeatedly affirming positive thoughts and emotions in order to dispel any negativity.

The advantages of employing optimistic self-verbalization

Undoubtedly, harnessing one's own abilities stands as the most significant means through which we can maximize our potential advantages in life.

Particularly, we can leverage our contemplations as they have an influence on our emotions and thereby

Lines have the potential to greatly impact our overall approach to life. By discovering methods of regulating our

Shifting one's internal dialogue and converting it into positive self-talk rather than negative, a practice that a majority of individuals can adopt.

The majority of individuals, without their awareness throughout the day, have the opportunity to commence managing various aspects of their lives.

and implement fundamental enhancements.

Your ability to succeed in life largely depends on your approach to life, a positive

A positive mindset ultimately leads to a confident and ultimately more successful person than someone who is filled with negativity.

characterized by a negative outlook, leading to a lack of courage and diminished self-esteem. By adopting a positive mindset, you approach life from a perspective different from that of negativity, an

Having a mindset of inspiration encourages the ability to perceive the greatness within individuals and the world, leading to

Exemplary dedication and accomplishment. Your personal contentment is contingent upon your cognitive and emotional state.

From moment to moment and altering your cognitive approach can profoundly influence your perspective.

Existence and effectively handle one's affairs.

An individual who approaches life with an optimistic mindset is more prepared to

effectively navigate through the challenges and adversities that life throws our way, they can rebound and recuperate

arising from difficulties or strategic actions in different aspects of life. The individual with idealistic tendencies will perceive the

The veracity concerning the matter, is merely a temporary setback from which they can recover and continue forward, once

By examining life through an optimistic lens, individuals can assert complete accountability for their actions.

they take into account their thoughts and feelings and turn a unfavorable situation into a progressively positive one

By effectively modifying their cognitive processes, individuals can cultivate a favorable mindset. Since contemplations can

Ensure or have a contrary stance, with only one concept maintained in utmost importance at any given moment.

Choosing to maintain a positive mindset during that period will enable you to cultivate optimistic thoughts, emotions, and behaviors, consequently leading to a greater sense of personal happiness and a more seamless attainment of your goals.

Confidence – Observation

The rationale behind my encouragement for you to observe others is rooted in the possibility that you may hold certain notions pertaining to the origin of your lack of confidence.

I am significantly overweight.
- I have an unattractive appearance
- I lack sufficient expertise or skill
- I lack the height necessary • I do not meet the required height • I fall short in terms of height

I am dissatisfied with my personal attire.

Indeed, it is beyond doubt that these sentiments have profound underpinnings that extend beyond the superficial assertions made earlier. However, it is evident that you possess notions and constructs pertaining to your perceived position within the broader framework. You perceive others as possessing greater physical attractiveness, a slimmer physique, a higher level of excellence compared to yourself, greater stature, or a superior sense of fashion. These disparaging remarks pertaining to your identity undermine your self-assurance. I aim to illustrate to you that one's physical appearance, including weight, attractiveness, abilities, height, or attire, holds no significance. Individuals of various body types possess self-assurance; thus, cease attributing your inadequacies and instead engage in attentive observation of those in your vicinity. For the purpose of this activity, make your way to the shopping mall or select an outdoor café where you can engage in observatory analysis of individuals.

In your observation, who do you believe embodies the highest level of self-assurance? What distinguished this individual from others? It is evident that individuals, irrespective of their physical attributes, demonstrate their confidence through their gait or manner upon entering a space. One observes their state of happiness, undoubtedly free from clumsiness or despondency. They will confront the world confidently and stand tall with their shoulders held erect. They exhibit no hesitancy in their approach towards individuals. The individual I encountered who exuded the greatest sense of self-assurance was a woman whose weight surpassed my own by twofold. Remarkably, she embraced herself entirely, demonstrating a profound contentment with her identity. It is imperative to comprehend that an individual, regardless of visual impairment, can emanate an aura of self-assurance when content with their own identity, even without the ability to visually perceive the garments they wear each morning. Confidence starts inside you. It is imperative that you grant yourself approval.

After carefully observing individuals, gain insight into their entry into the room, paying particular attention to the contrasting behaviors exhibited by those who exude confidence and those who lack it. Individuals who possess self-assurance radiate a remarkable presence in comparison to those burdened by self-doubt. They do not harbor insecurities regarding their size and instead carry themselves with a sense of dignity and self-assurance. The issue lies in the fact that contemporary society has imposed certain expectations upon your schedule. One can observe flawless models featured in catalogs. One observes individuals who consistently experience greater fortune than oneself or those who exhibit a state of happiness and contentment in their existence. Allow me to present a candid reality. If you fail to modify your methodology, you will not attract individuals into your life who will contribute to your overall happiness. The concept of the Law of Attraction is based on the principle of vibrations, whereby individuals who possess a negative and self-conscious disposition emit unfavorable vibrations that inevitably attract similar negative vibrations. Certainly, an individual may exhibit kindness towards you, but is it preferable for them to display this kindness as a result of sympathizing with your circumstances? Wouldn't it be more favorable if they harbored authentic positive sentiments towards you, prompted by their genuine fondness for you? When one increases their determination and cultivates a positive mindset, they possess the ability to err numerous times yet still earn the affection and admiration of others.

Dressing to kill

It is evident through careful observation that an individual's level of success and self-confidence is directly influenced by the manner in which they project their image to the world. You observed it. Therefore, let us examine the contents of your wardrobe and identify the garments in which you experience joy and comfort. Wearing attire that is inadequately sized due to concerns regarding the visibility of labels on oversized garments is unlikely to yield any advantages for yourself. If this holds significant importance to you, I would suggest having your measurements taken for undergarments and if necessary, discreetly remove the size label from the underwear. Women who don ill-fitting bras invariably experience discomfort and convey an air of unease. They exhibit protrusions in unexpected anatomical areas. Likewise, gentlemen who don attire in ill-suited trousers or pants appear conspicuously inappropriate. A properly proportioned waistline contributes to the individual's overall comfort, eliminating the need for constant self-adjustment and self-consciousness. Therefore, adopt a strategic approach to dressing, beginning with the foundational garments, and ensure that every item you choose to don instills within you a sense of confidence.

Proceed into your bedroom, heading towards the full-length mirror, and gracefully present yourself while adorned in the attire you have carefully selected that instills a sense of confidence and self-assurance. Clothes are not you. Nevertheless, these factors ultimately contribute to initial perceptions. In the event that one's self-assurance is deficient, presenting a polished appearance, with well-groomed hair, a fresh complexion, clean hands, and an overall impression of self-care, significantly enhances the likelihood of making a favorable impression. When an individual engages in nail biting, wears soiled footwear, and fails to exhibit proper personal care, it forms an initial perception among others that suggests insecurity. A lack of confidence does not contribute positively to one's perception of oneself. Hence, one's external appearance holds significance. If one were to deliver a speech while wearing trousers that are snug around the waist and shoes that cause instability, one would inevitably divert attention towards oneself and become noticeable by the audience. Subsequently, one becomes aware of the expressions directed towards oneself and internalizes a sense of pessimism, resulting in detrimental effects on one's self-confidence. By exerting the necessary efforts to address any potential visual concerns others may harbor towards you, you will enhance your likelihood of projecting an air of confidence and effectively presenting yourself in a manner that is widely accepted as customary.

Introversion And Its Impact On Interpersonal Relationships

Challenges Encountered in Interpersonal Relationships: Practical Strategies for Enhancing Connections (Both Platonic and Romantic, Suitable for Both Genders)

Therefore, this circumstance implies that the introvert may be compelled to venture outside of their comfort zones in order to uphold and preserve the relationships they have established, which hold significant importance to them.

The aspect inherent in introverted individuals is that, predominantly, they frequently cultivate associations that they seek to establish. The individuals whom they choose to keep in their company, the individuals with whom they associate, are typically individuals whom the introvert desires to have in their presence.

In a manner similar to any interpersonal connection, individuals with introverted tendencies will invariably encounter relationship challenges. However, in your particular scenario, your inclination towards introversion introduces a layer of complexity. For example;

Varied Modes of Communication

How frequently have conflicts arisen between yourself and the individuals within your social circle? In all candor, on several occasions if the relationship is in good health.

Now, when considering matters from your vantage point, it is commonplace for you to briefly immerse yourself in contemplation following a bout of disagreement. As a consequence, the individual in your life might interpret this as an indication that you are evading them, whereas in actuality, you are devoting time, as is customary for you, to analyze your thoughts and reflections.

Individuals with extroverted tendencies frequently observe that they exhibit enhanced responsiveness within a dynamically rapid environment. If one is an introvert and embarks on a romantic relationship with an extrovert, the divergent modes of communication employed by both individuals may engender certain tensions and conflicts within the relationship.

Establishing effective communication is a fundamental component of fostering a strong and harmonious interpersonal connection. Hence, being an introvert naturally entails a propensity to immerse oneself in introspection and indulge in the creation of intricate mental constructs. Consequently, this inclination can devalue and downplay the significance of tangible relationships, ultimately culminating in a discordant breakdown in communication - this being merely the initial phase of a progressive deterioration in the quality of the connection.

As previously indicated, it should be noted that certain individuals who possess introverted traits may also experience shyness. Consequently, this could result in heightened challenges when it comes to efficient communication due to diminished self-assurance and heightened social anxiety. This scenario possesses the potential to erode the foundations of the relationship.

Silence may be misinterpreted amidst a conflict.

In how many instances of conflict have you found yourself engaged? In all likelihood, it is safe to assume that it has occurred on multiple occasions, correct?

The matter at hand is that, due to their reserved and tranquil nature, introverts frequently refrain from manifesting their complete spectrum of emotions. When experiencing anger, individuals often exhibit a composed demeanor and instead of erupting (unless provoked significantly), introverted individuals have a tendency to maintain a tranquil disposition and engage in reflective contemplation. Have you accomplished it, per chance?

Presently, a considerable number of individuals in this vicinity exhibit extroverted tendencies. They comprehend that conflict entails reciprocal engagement between individuals, with both parties actively involved in confronting each other. Nevertheless, in your particular circumstance, your reticence and composure could be interpreted as indifference or a manifestation of disregard for the viewpoints expressed by others. If you are at work and it is your boss confronting you, you may inexplicably be giving off the vibe that you do not take what they are saying seriously.

In the event of a disagreement with your significant other, it is possible that you may unintentionally convey an air of arrogance or indifference towards them, despite there being no basis for such assumptions. Failure to exercise proper care may result in a breakdown of communication, subsequently posing a risk to the integrity of your relationships, which hold great significance to you.

Divergent Interests within Your Partner/Friends

When engaging in a romantic relationship with an individual who possesses a higher level of extroversion, it is likely that your respective personalities may intersect and converge.

There you find yourself, having become accustomed to cherishing moments of solitude, cozily nestled on a couch, engrossed in a book or film. Once you enter into a committed partnership, the need to arrange outings with your significant other arises.

Whilst these variations may be resolved through effective communication, it is not uncommon to experience a sense of discontentment while striving to increase social engagement and extroversion. As a consequence, conflicts between partners may arise frequently.

In the event that you and your partner engage in a social outing where they find it necessary to capture a photograph, it will be incumbent upon you to fulfill this obligation, irrespective of any personal discomfort you may experience. Such circumstances are perpetual, often culminating in discord.

You are not fond of discussing your personal matters.

Envision yourself embarking on an inaugural romantic rendezvous. Indeed, the sight of butterflies and all the excitement aside, one quickly acknowledges their hesitancy in engaging in self-disclosure to this unfamiliar individual. Despite having gone on a few dates, it is possible that you may still not feel at ease.

The inclination of introverts to maintain a certain level of privacy frequently results in the detriment of their relationships.

In order to establish and cultivate relationships, it is imperative that we adopt a willingness to embrace vulnerability when interacting with the other party. This enhances the cultivation of trust and facilitates the development of stronger personal connections.

While individuals who are introverted may appreciate the opportunity to establish profound connections with others, it is their tendency to deliberately limit the disclosure of personal information. Typically, individuals do not have ulterior motives prompting their actions. It is possible that they experience a sense of being overwhelmed or have not yet fully immersed themselves in the relationship. Introverted individuals tend to invest a substantial amount of time in cultivating relationships, which may consequently give rise to a challenging situation for their extroverted companions or significant others.

Due to your evident reluctance in engaging in personal discourse, it is possible that you may inadvertently convey a sense of disinterest, thereby leading the individual to interpret this as an indication of their diminished significance in your estimation.

Over-Thinking

Indeed, engaging in thoughtful reflection is truly commendable! Your exemplary grasp of this concept is most impressive. However, excessive use can give rise to complications, much like any other situation.

The inherent inclination of an introverted individual to immerse themselves in intricacies, strategizing, observing, and deciphering often leads them to approach almost every situation with a cognitive frame of mind.

When engaging in the act of shopping, one tends to fixate or become preoccupied with the decisions that must be made. The jam is excessively sweetened, however, the desired marmalade is currently out of stock. The substitute jelly appears appealing, although it originates from an unfamiliar brand; however, the third choice holds potential. The fourth alternative bears a resemblance to an inexpensive imitation of your favorite choice. The fifth choice is situated significantly lower in the list, and so forth.

This matter can prove to be exasperating for individuals who are present in your social circle. Due to your quest for making sound judgments, your preoccupation with minutiae could potentially foster a disconnect between yourself and the individuals in your vicinity.

In this instance, this situation could potentially result in the alienation of your friends and associates, as a consequence of your transition into being perceived as uninteresting.

While it may be perceived as being shallow and self-absorbed, excessive rumination could prove to be unproductive in the foreseeable future since it entails becoming entangled in the dilemma of options, potentially leading to the selection of a subpar alternative.

You Struggle in A Group Setting

As previously mentioned, as an introvert, you derive significant solace from being in your own company. During solitary moments, which often constitute a significant portion of one's time, individuals engage in brainstorming, conceiving narratives, and producing visual artwork. You engage in the exploration and contemplation of thoughts, ideas, and concepts. Fundamentally, you transform into your principal repository of knowledge.

However, subsequent to that, when one engages in social activities with one's acquaintances, one discovers oneself to be a constituent of a collective. Abruptly, the chambers of your thoughts are sealed. The narratives you desired to convey are confined within. Amidst the presence of numerous individuals, the constant interactions deplete one's energy reserves. Incapable of accessing your introspective musings, you assume a reticent demeanor within the collective, leaving the impression of being a mere bystander. Your acquaintances are developing the belief that you do not hold the relationship in high regard, despite your repeated reassurances. It appears that your actions are incongruous with your verbal expressions.

Being an introvert entails experiencing difficulty in navigating circumstances that valorize extroversion.

Consequently, this may lead to the emergence of tensions in your social relationships. You will exhibit an air of aloofness and apparent reluctance to engage in social interactions, despite the fact that your true limitation lies in the difficulty of accessing your optimal thoughts within a group dynamic. This can also be exasperating for you, given your introverted disposition. You are unable to provide a satisfactory explanation for your lack of ability to engage in proficient group thinking. Therefore, establishing a meaningful connection with others becomes challenging.

In the context of a romantic relationship, when your partner perceives that you derive greater satisfaction from solitude than from being in their company, they may instinctively withdraw, understanding that you do not depend on their presence.

In order to mitigate the occurrences described, what potential resolutions might be considered?

Strategies for Cultivating Stronger Interpersonal Connections for Individuals with Introverted Characteristics

Embrace Yourself

Due to the cynicism associated with introverts, certain individuals may resort to drastic measures in order to project a false extroverted persona, thereby seeking validation from others.

It is evident that you are initiating the path towards failure in this relationship by assuming a false identity, an act that can be described as displaying a lack of honesty. In addition to this, however, you will encounter difficulty expressing your emotions effectively, thereby necessitating a steadfast commitment to avoid compromising your integrity. This ongoing incident persists until it reaches a juncture where one's tolerance is exhausted, resulting in a sudden and forceful reaction. Circumstances undergo abrupt shifts, and as a consequence, your interpersonal connections teeter on the verge of disintegration, delicately poised upon the brink of an abyss.

You can avoid this. In order to cultivate stronger relationships, it is often recommended by relationship experts that one first establishes a foundation of self-love. As an individual with introverted tendencies, this will require accepting and acknowledging your introversion, while also gaining insight into your own communication style and preferences, as well as establishing expectations for how others should communicate with you. What is the manner in which you most effectively feel and express love? Could you please enlighten me on the manner in which you express your discontent? What forms of positive reinforcement do you employ, and which ones do you value when received from others? What are your preferences regarding physical contact? Which specific gestures are you seeking? Gifts? Words?

Only by attaining a sense of self-assurance can one progress towards the subsequent stages.

Leverage Your Aptitude for Active Listening

This particular aptitude serves as a primary asset amidst your introverted nature. Therefore, it has the potential to be an effective instrument for establishing stronger connections with individuals whom you engage or encounter.

However, in order to further develop upon this point, it is advantageous to engage in active listening by paraphrasing the speaker's remarks after they have concluded their statements. By employing this proactive approach, you can effectively assess your listening skills, all while communicating to the speaker that their words are being attentively heard. Individuals frequently develop a deeper sense of connection with others who foster their feelings of worthiness. By paraphrasing the thoughts expressed by the other individual (while making necessary adjustments), you subtly convey your appreciation and enthusiasm for continued engagement with them. You will discover that by authentically being yourself, rather than adopting an extroverted or loud persona, you will cultivate stronger interpersonal connections.

Furthermore, be attentive in order to acquire knowledge about the individual. You will be astounded by the expeditiousness with which this will facilitate the establishment of a connection with them.

Occasionally Acknowledge Party Invitations

Indeed, I am cognizant of how this might unsettle you, however, it is worth noting that social circles are typically formed and upheld through regular and frequent interactions among individuals. When one possesses companions and they make a concerted effort to incorporate one into social gatherings, it would behoove one to collaboratively decide upon the manner of accepting said invitations.

In order to foster robust affiliations with individuals, maintaining transparency will facilitate a scenario wherein they can proffer you an invitation, allowing you to accept or decline selectively, or conceivably accept all and subsequently negotiate an early departure.

We all derive great benefit from interpersonal connections, so it is advisable to avoid excessive self-isolation. Please consider accepting occasional invitations, ensuring that your mental well-being is not compromised in the process. Your acquaintances should demonstrate the ability to uphold the mutually agreed-upon boundaries, and you reciprocally do likewise.

Exhibit Compassion towards Unfamiliar Individuals

Primarily, it is imperative that we exhibit kindness towards all individuals. However, in general, numerous individuals frequently display impoliteness towards unfamiliar individuals unwarrantedly. As a result, it has become customary for many individuals to display indifference and disdain towards strangers in certain situations.

As an individual who identifies as an introvert and is striving to cultivate stronger interpersonal connections, it may prove beneficial to adopt an alternative approach – exhibiting genuine kindness towards unfamiliar individuals. What this accomplishes is the facilitation of recognizing the inherent human qualities possessed by the other individual. By expressing gratitude towards the cashier, you demonstrate their significance. By granting clemency to the individual who inadvertently caused you offense, you convey your acknowledgement of the fallibility inherent to human beings.

When in the company of your companions, this will facilitate a stronger sense of connection and foster a desire for affiliation with you. You are likely to gain their admiration, which may lead to an increased desire to associate with you.

Conversely, by demonstrating kindness towards others, you will amass an extensive network of potential friends, thereby enhancing your social prospects. As you choose to undertake this gesture of your own accord, free from any obligation to please others, you are likely to derive pleasure from it. Moreover, it will afford you the opportunity to develop a more insightful understanding of the desires and necessities of individuals. Despite the efficacy of your actions falling short, you can take solace in the certainty of having given your utmost effort.

Engage in casual conversation related to subjects that hold your interest

Engaging in casual conversation can sometimes be tedious. That fact has been firmly established. Frequently employed as a means to fill uncomfortable pauses, it frequently exhibits heightened levels of awkwardness, lackluster quality, superficiality, and absence of purpose. For an introspective individual who exercises caution in their speech and reflective in their thoughts, such musings undeniably elicit a strong desire for exasperation.

Nevertheless, although it is indisputable that small conversations often prove to be less than satisfactory, the underlying issue does not solely lie within the concept of small talk itself; rather, it primarily derives from the fact that a significant number of individuals, both introverted and extroverted, struggle with communication skills.

Consequently, you will discover that your aversion lies not so much in the notion of engaging in casual conversations, but rather in the sentiment of them being contrived and lacking authenticity.

Hence, allocate a moment to contemplate the manner in which you desire individuals to engage in casual conversations with you, considering the appropriate setting and approach. If you have the opportunity to initiate contact, please proceed. This methodology could potentially be easily attained by participating in an event that aligns with your personal interests or holds significant value to you.

To accomplish this, allocate an appropriate amount of time to the task. Do not hastily proceed solely in pursuit of expeditious completion. Allow yourself the opportunity to further acclimate to the notion of engaging in social interaction by venturing outside to initiate a dialogue.

This statement does not imply that you will transform into an individual who actively engages with others, but rather suggests that you will develop the ability to discern when and how to initiate such interactions, thereby securing your comfort in the process.

Understanding Body Language

Nonverbal cues constitute a primary means of communication, surpassing other forms of interaction in the amount of information they convey. A person's physique remains honest; in the event of their agitation, their physicality will unequivocally reveal it. Should they become displeased, their physiological signs will manifest it. The human body can effectively manifest signs indicating exhaustion, engagement, ennui, and other related states to reflect an individual's desires and inclinations.

Non-verbal communication plays a pivotal role in our day-to-day exchanges and engagements. It is highly likely that you are already observing and analyzing a significantly greater amount of body language than you may believe. If one observes a distinct swaying of the hips in another individual while walking, it may provide sufficient insight into their intentions and desires. A subtle shift in the direction of the eyes can significantly signify nonverbal communication. These movements are of a highly nuanced nature and lead to the conveyance of ideas and attitudes.

If you possess any background in acting or improvisation, you are likely aware that an individual's body language can provide insight into their character traits. If an individual "takes the lead" with a specific body part, you may observe that it manifests in their gait; for instance, one person may take the lead with their head, which becomes the most conspicuous body part as they move about. An alternative approach could involve emphasizing the movements originating from the hips. Individuals have a tendency to highlight a specific region of their physique during ambulation, which can provide some insights into their character traits. As an illustration, suppose an individual's predominant movement pattern involves leading with their hips. This could suggest that they possess a heightened sensuality and enlivened sexuality, which greatly influence their demeanor and guide their actions in the physical and mental realms. Should an individual approach a situation by relying on their intellect, it is conceivable that they possess a proclivity for employing their cognitive abilities to address a dilemma. If an individual demonstrates a preference for leading with their feet, it could indicate a tendency towards caution, implying a reluctance to hastily engage in matters and a preference for revealing themselves only when the situation appears safe and secure.

All these illustrations demonstrate the various methodologies employed for the analysis of nonverbal communication. It is important to consider that body language is a form of art, both in its expression and interpretation. It is imperative that you employ strategic and shrewd discernment while dealing with this matter. Formulas do not exist; rather, intuition is the sole determinant. It is imperative to cultivate the aspect within yourself that possesses the ability to instinctively discern individuals and rely upon the corresponding facet of your cognitive process. Identifiable archetypes can be sought out to facilitate the interpretation of body language. These are archetypes in which individuals manifest their personalities. Occasionally, their statements are correct; however, on certain occasions, there may be additional nuances to consider.

Primarily, we have the archetype commonly referred to as the "police officer." The archetype of the "police officer" can be observed in parents, figures of authority, and individuals who evoke feelings of intimidation. The police officer's stance exudes an imposing presence, characterized by an upright posture, an expanded chest, and a dignified alignment of the head and neck. The core muscles of a police officer should consistently be strengthened and engaged, while maintaining preparedness to quickly access tools positioned at the waist. This stance is indicative of a state of vigilance, assertiveness, and resilience. This conceptual prototype can be invoked to recall the nonverbal communication traits exhibited by an individual who aligns with these archetypal patterns. The countenance will exude a demeanor of sternness and seriousness. The leader may venture into the matter, yet stays consistently vigilant.

The subsequent persona embodying nonverbal communication is the intellectual. The individual referred to as a "nerd" tends to display inherent submissive tendencies, particularly in unfamiliar settings, and consistently exhibits a propensity towards self-protection. The individual possesses shoulders that lack muscular development and fail to exude physical prowess. Eye contact is infrequently established with individuals of this nature. The intellectual individual will consistently seek methods to disengage, exhibit avoidance, avert their gaze, or relocate their body elsewhere to evade interaction with the majority of individuals in society. The individual of scholarly inclination lacks proficiency in social engagement. Nevertheless, when the individual with scholarly inclinations is immersed in their domain, they will project a magnified and robust presence. Individuals may exhibit an alternative demeanor when in the presence of individuals they have confidence in or when engaged in activities that bring them pleasure. This pertains to deciphering non-verbal cues, enabling the recognition of whether a person is comfortable and confident, or uncomfortable and ill at ease.

A supplementary archetype worth considering is the "femme fatale." The femme fatale personifies the notion that she possesses that which all desire. Although they may exhibit a demure demeanor in their verbal expression, their non-verbal cues convey a high level of implication. They may opt to don attire that highlights their physique, and they may derive pleasure from enticing and manipulating others through the deliberate exposure of specific body parts to select individuals. The enchantress will possess an acute awareness of the opportune moments to unveil their presence to those in their vicinity, as well as when it is prudent to maintain silence. They possess great adeptness in achieving their goals, skillfully employing their attractiveness as a means to attain what they desire. The individual in question exhibits pronounced body language traits, such as frequent tactile contact and close spatial proximity. The enchantress will possess the skill to convey a tangible feeling of intimacy to those individuals whom they desire to associate with, and they will actively seek a connection with nearly all individuals they wish to engage with. They possess a tendency to adeptly manipulate individuals, particularly those who experience feelings of isolation or apprehension. Frequently, they will initiate movement by positioning their hips or showcasing their breasts, both of which will be readily apparent in a given location. These individuals have a propensity for making a grand entrance. You will become cognizant of their presence upon their entrance to a room.

An additional embodiment of body language archetype is the portrayal of the "elderly woman." This archetype signifies the conventional representation of a mature lady who has fulfilled her life's obligations and carries a sense of utmost contentment. This individual possesses a keen awareness of her inherent grace and elegance, coupled with a wealth of profound experiences.

Nevertheless, her primary focus does not revolve around attaining her desires, given that she has largely achieved her desired outcomes throughout her life. The elderly woman expresses contentment and displays an increased interest in social engagement. She will display a strong inclination towards maintaining eye contact and smiling, accompanied by vibrant facial expressions that indicate her genuine delight upon encountering another individual. She will exhibit elegant leadership through her hips, yet maintain a restrained approach. One aspect worth observing in the body language of this particular archetype is their facial expression, as individuals in advanced age frequently exhibit a diminished range of emotional display.

Another exemplification of nonverbal communication is the "humble worker" archetype. The humble worker understands their position within the hierarchy and possesses the ability to exhibit nonverbal gestures that convey respect towards those in their immediate vicinity. These individuals may encompass those who they are employed by or collaborating with. The diligent employee seldom diverts their attention from their tasks, yet on the occasions they do, they shall unveil their demeanor, offering insight into their inner disposition. The demeanor of a modest employee might align with their circumstances, suggesting they may belong to a category of workers who do not derive satisfaction from socializing. In this particular scenario, a diligent employee will refrain from establishing visual contact, instead placing greater emphasis on the diligent execution of their assigned tasks. Nevertheless, individuals exhibiting characteristics indicative of this particular form of non-verbal communication tend to excel in the ability to make eye contact, engage in smiling, and derive pleasure from social interactions. The individual's stance might be hunched over, as they dedicate a significant portion of their time to diligent work. These individuals might demonstrate a tendency to prioritize manual activities, given that working with their hands is a prevalent interest among them.

Advantages Derived from Enhancing Self-Esteem and Self-Confidence

At this juncture within the book, you have acquired knowledge regarding the adverse consequences brought about by low self-esteem, as well as its prevailing origins. Now, we shall proceed towards exploring the advantages associated with enhancing one's self-esteem and self-confidence. As previously indicated, self-esteem and self-confidence are closely intertwined, and each one exerts a direct influence on the other. The absence of robust self-esteem renders the acquisition of necessary self-assurance for accomplishing desired objectives in life a considerably arduous endeavor. Through acquiring knowledge about the advantages associated with a robust sense of self-worth, one can initiate the exploration of incentives and commence the adoption of methodologies aimed at enhancing self-esteem. Please be aware that although enhancing one's self-esteem in later stages of life may present greater challenges, it is not an insurmountable endeavor. Similar to the majority of endeavors in existence, it necessitates diligent effort and dedication towards essential facets such as cultivating self-consciousness and embracing oneself. For individuals who have young children or intend to have children, it is essential to bear in mind that the development of self-esteem during the formative stages of a child's life is highly susceptible to external influences. Please ensure that you remain cognizant of the environment you are cultivating for your children, and bear in mind the significance of instilling a sense of worth and esteem in them. By instilling in them a robust sense of self-worth from an early age, they can develop into individuals who are self-assured in their capabilities and aspirations. We shall commence our session by exploring the advantages that arise from possessing a robust sense of self-worth, and subsequently, we shall proceed to delve into the merits associated with self-assurance.

Advantages of Enhancing Self-Esteem

The following are the five advantages that are associated with enhancing self-esteem:

• Self-confidence enhances your level of assertiveness.

• Self-esteem enhances one's sense of assurance in the process of decision-making.

• Self-esteem fosters a sense of emotional stability, trustworthiness, and integrity within interpersonal connections.

- A diminished sense of self-worth decreases the probability of remaining in a detrimental partnership.
- Self-esteem aids in the cultivation of realistic assessments of oneself and others
- The development of a positive self-image enhances an individual's ability to cope with and overcome stressful situations and challenges.

Enhancing Self-Esteem Enhances Assertiveness

Assertiveness is an indispensable skill that individuals must possess in order to maintain equilibrium in their lives. When an individual possesses self-esteem, it greatly aids them in cultivating unwavering conviction in their words, actions, and inquiries. If an individual harbors a belief regarding their desires or requirements, it becomes unnecessary for them to dedicate their cognitive faculties to ascertain the consensus on its veracity. Individuals with diminished self-regard encounter difficulties in displaying assertiveness due to their apprehension of being evaluated or turned down. They believe that the act of seeking assistance is indicative of vulnerability, leading to potential scrutiny and criticism for expressing their needs. Contrarily, an individual possessing a robust self-image harbors no apprehension while expressing their needs, as any sense of uncertainty or doubt is absent. Self-esteem arises from an inherent love and regard for oneself; hence, individuals who possess this self-care exhibit a high degree of normalcy in expressing their desires and requirements.

To further elucidate the concept of assertiveness, I shall furnish you with a straightforward illustration. Envisage a situation wherein your maternal figure requests your prompt presence at her residence to assist in the process of packing and relocating her belongings in preparation for her imminent move. Nevertheless, due to the challenging week you have endured at your workplace, you have made prior arrangements to dedicate your evening to serene pursuits such as indulging in a film and enjoying a rejuvenating soak in a warm bath. In this instance, assertiveness refers to the ability to regard one's own needs with equal importance as those of others, such as that of one's mother. In this scenario, an individual possessing a robust sense of self-worth would assert, "I am deserving and entitled to this respite as I am well aware of its necessity for my well-being." Conversely, someone afflicted with diminished self-esteem might express, "Indulging in a tranquil evening would be an act of selfishness on my part, particularly when there is someone seeking my assistance." Recognizing that it is impossible to offer support or aid when one's own reserves are depleted is a key tenet of cultivating healthy self-esteem. In the given illustration, assuming an individual possesses diminished self-esteem, it is likely that they will proceed to assist their mother in relocating, irrespective of experiencing significant fatigue. Consequently, they will eventually harbor sentiments of being undervalued by others. Nevertheless, individuals can only grasp one's emotions when they effectively express their feelings, thereby absolving the mother of any blame for merely seeking assistance.

Allow me to present an additional demonstration of assertiveness. On this occasion, the illustration will pertain to the professional milieu. Consider a scenario in which your employer, for the third occasion within this month, requests your assistance in completing your colleague's report due to the latter's recurring delays. Furthermore, your employer acknowledges your superior work ethic and proficiency in comparison to said colleague. An individual characterized by a strong sense of self-worth would respond as follows, "Within the span of this month, you have thrice approached me to undertake additional responsibilities due to John's recurring delays." I place great importance on fostering a spirit of collaboration and teamwork; however, I experience heightened levels of stress and overwhelm when constantly burdened with additional responsibilities. "What measures should we implement to ensure the recurrence of such incidents is prevented?" This is the recommended approach to address your supervisor in this scenario, as it is essential to assert oneself and communicate that a line has been crossed, expressing dissatisfaction with consistently being exploited. An individual characterized by diminished self-esteem in such a circumstance would probably acquiesce to assume the additional workload, albeit gradually fostering feelings of resentment towards their colleague. It is probable that they will become excessively depleted as a result of the additional workload, ultimately attributing blame to others and thereby nurturing dysfunctional interpersonal dynamics. Engaging in effective communication with others and expressing your emotions provides an opportunity for individuals to comprehend your perspective and modify their behaviors accordingly.

Acquiring the ability to effectively assert oneself is an indispensable life skill that holds great significance, owing to its extensive application and the level of admiration it commands. If one believes they are afflicted by the "yes" syndrome, it may be advantageous for them to prioritize the development of their self-esteem in order to enhance their ability to acknowledge and honor their own desires and requirements. It is important to bear in mind that there is a distinction between assertiveness and aggression. In the realm of interpersonal dynamics, assertiveness encompasses the crucial quality of expressing one's desires and requirements in a resolute and unmistakable manner, whereas aggression primarily centers around the forceful and imperious nature of making demands. The manner in which an individual conveys their message, employing both vocal intonation and nonverbal cues, significantly impacts the manner in which individuals interpret your appeal.

The Rationale Behind Establishing Objectives

It is imperative to acknowledge that when establishing objectives for oneself, these goals fall beyond one's sphere of influence. Consequently, excessive dedication to the pursuit of these goals can hinder their realization. In contrast, by directing your attention towards your actions rather than your objectives, you can attain your goals.

Only you have the ability to observe and manage your actions. They are under your control. Therefore, it is necessary to disregard the aspects of your objectives that are beyond your control and concentrate on the aspects that are within your sphere of influence, namely your actions. Once you focus on your actions, day after day, you begin to learn all the information you need to reach your set goals.

When one considers their goal as already accomplished, it places them in a position whereby they can direct their attention towards formulating a plan to actualize it. Behaviors exhibit a short-term orientation when goals are established, typically within a span of seven days. Therefore, one must consider the actions one can undertake in the present day, following through with them in the subsequent days and throughout the current week by documenting and pursuing them diligently.

The Art of Defining Precise Objectives

It is advisable to demonstrate sagacity, as the current reality is intricately rooted in your past, in the form of your prior experiences. If one constrains their future prospects based on their past experiences, their progress will be hindered. It is imperative to establish aspirations of sufficient magnitude to propel oneself forward. Therefore, refrain from halting and asking, "What is the methodology behind this?"

It is not the first step. The first stage entails documenting all the necessary information, and by doing so, you have the ability to fashion and mold your own personal utopia, according to your preferences. It commences with a straightforward procedure of extracting these widely stated dream impulses and subsequently refining them with greater precision.

This demonstrates the efficacy of setting goals. There is a deeper comprehension concerning the act of documenting thoughts in writing. Something happens. You embody the role of a creator when you establish objectives and document them in writing. You acquire a lucid vision and possess the ability to translate it into reality.

As a result, it is imperative to ensure that you not only establish objectives, but also gain a comprehensive understanding of the underlying motivations behind them. It is irrefutable that goal-setting possesses an inherent essence capable of transforming one's life, with the resounding truth being that purpose holds greater power than the ultimate result.

The rationale behind establishing goals

The essence of this statement is that the underlying significance of setting goals lies not in the attainment of material possessions, but rather in the transformative impact they have on one's character and personal growth. I am currently experiencing the phase of realization. Many individuals establish goals without careful consideration." "Most people establish goals without conducting thorough analysis." "The majority of individuals set goals haphazardly." "A large percentage of people set goals without due diligence. They possess a strong inclination towards and prioritize material possessions. There is no inherent issue with that; I encourage you to possess as many things as you desire, as it is a natural aspect of life.

It constitutes an integral component of the manifestation process in achieving desired outcomes through goal-setting. If one's sole preoccupation is solely centered upon attaining material possessions, it could potentially jeopardize one's inherent moral principles and the pursuit of one's desired personal and creative expressions in life. One must exercise caution.

While the prospect of earning money may provide some level of motivation, experiencing both financial and physical abundance and being able to manifest this abundance not only for oneself but also for others is a far more fulfilling endeavor. Possessing the unrestricted financial capability or bestowing it upon others through acts of generosity typically serves as a greater source of motivation than anything else.

Developing Self-Love

While it is commonly asserted that individuals with low self-esteem ought to cultivate self-love, it is frequently observed that such individuals tend to disregard this guidance due to their perception of the notion as unfamiliar or perplexing. Nevertheless, it is the sole affection upon which you can unequivocally rely in the entirety of your existence. When one possesses the capability to embrace self-love, individuals in one's vicinity commence to identify elements of merit within oneself that warrant their affection. Consider it in this manner. If one does not possess self-love, it becomes implausible for others to reciprocate affection towards them. It is illogical to anticipate individuals to have affection towards someone whom you intensely dislike. That is the aspect that individuals lacking in self-confidence fail to grasp. It is comparatively more straightforward to transition from one unfavorable relationship to another, seeking approval from an individual who fails to perceive you as a peer. You must elevate your standards and commence acknowledging your true identity and personal convictions within the realm of existence. Cease succumbing to the influence of others in determining the course of your life and commence pursuing your own aspirations.

Strategy 4 – Identifying one's personal passions and areas of interest
Numerous individuals derive enjoyment from engaging in the act of listening to music. Several individuals will derive pleasure from the experience of viewing an outstanding film. However, there are individuals who derive pleasure from indulging in a relaxing soak or pampering themselves with a facial treatment. It is crucial for you to take the time to introspect and determine your personal sources of joy, subsequently incorporating a practice of indulging in activities that bring you genuine

satisfaction on a daily basis. It assists in fostering a stronger sense of self by enabling individuals to engage in activities without succumbing to external influences, thereby allowing them to experience enjoyment without experiencing any semblance of guilt. It is not imperative for it to be characterized by a high cost. Compose a record enumerating the activities that genuinely provide you with satisfaction and ensure that one of these is integrated into your daily routine henceforth. It is necessary to cultivate a deep appreciation for one's own identity.

All individuals possess an inner child, and occasionally allowing that aspect of oneself to surface can prove beneficial. As an example, should you have a preference for engaging in game activities or seeking comfort with a plush toy, feel free to indulge in such pursuits. If one derives pleasure from engaging in recreational activities, it is advisable to pursue them. While you may not possess exceptional culinary skills, there is no harm in indulging in the creation of a distinguished confectionary masterpiece such as a gingerbread house. Even if your execution falls short, this endeavor will provide an opportunity to embrace your inner child. Allow him/her to do so as it enhances the quality of life and brings about a sense of enjoyment.

Strategic Approach 5 – Exercising Awareness

Individuals who experience self-esteem challenges often reflect upon past remarks directed towards them, resulting in negative emotions. It is inherent to their disposition. In the context of this approach, you relinquish attachment to prior circumstances. It is essential for you to anchor your focus and awareness in the present moment. This implies that whenever you observe your thoughts drifting towards the past, you promptly redirect your focus to the present moment. Do not harbor self-resentment for contemplating past occurrences, rather, promptly cease this pattern, as it is liable to exacerbate further complications. Alternatively, acknowledge the presence of the thought and leverage it to stimulate a constructive course of action. For instance, when considering a past romantic relationship that caused emotional distress, it is imperative to extract oneself from that situation and engage in an introspective assessment of one's surroundings. Please illustrate the mental images that you perceive. It is considerably more advantageous to focus on positive experiences rather than dwelling on past traumas, as it has a significantly greater impact on personal well-being compared to reflecting on one's past. Cease dwelling on the past and relinquish concerns for the future. It hasn't happened yet. Redirect your focus to the present moment and consciously reorient yourself to it whenever previous criticisms resurface in your thoughts.

The difficulty inherent in this situation lies in the fact that each time you entertain these thoughts and allow them to concern you, you are essentially affirming the veracity of someone's statements. Stop it. It's only a thought. Utilize it as a catalyst for the promotion of introspection. Observe your surroundings at this present moment and take notice of the radiant sunlight. Observe the blossoms within the park. Observe the expressions of contentment displayed on individuals' countenances and desist from engaging in self-destructive behavior that undermines your own existence. Each instance in which you engage in such behavior serves to further exacerbate your underlying self-esteem challenges. The exacerbation stems from the fact that you are magnifying the significance of the previous occurrence. The individual who inflicted harm upon you in the past is no longer experiencing any repercussions. Thus, why should you?

If your parents exhibited a tendency to offer unfavorable evaluations during your formative years, it is highly likely that they were oblivious to their actions. Cease grasping onto these items. Inhale through the nasal passages, and exhale while simultaneously considering the significant aspects of the present moment. Substitute pessimistic thoughts with enjoyable thoughts. Observe the children enthusiastically moving about in the park. Look at nature. Embark on a journey through the enchanting forest and witness the marvels of nature from up close. Cease indulging in retrospection, as it proves unproductive, fostering negativity and self-criticism in your psyche.

It is imperative to employ mindfulness in a highly constructive manner. What I teach people is to recognize when they are confronted by a situation that is too difficult and how to move forward. The primary objective is to relinquish the assumption that one is incapable of achieving it. The subsequent step entails inquiring with an individual regarding the methodology employed. All individuals acquire knowledge and skills, though at times, individuals may require further guidance. In the event of any confusion, I would encourage you to inquire about the aspect that is causing perplexity, thereby abstaining from adopting a mindset of incompetence. You simply haven't acquired the ability to cultivate an awareness of the individuals around you who may take pleasure in imparting new knowledge to you. They might derive the same degree of satisfaction from offering their assistance voluntarily that you derive from offering your assistance in distinct situations.

In the following chapter, we will address specific considerations that must be taken into account in the pursuit of attaining confidence. This chapter will serve as a comprehensive guide that encapsulates the steps necessary for you to cultivate the desired level of confidence.

Joy And Self-Recognition Function In Tandem.

Accepting Oneself

While there is a connection between the two, it is important to note that self-acknowledgment and self-esteem are distinct concepts. While self-esteem refers to the perception of our own importance or usefulness, self-acknowledgment implies a more assertive recognition of one's own truth or existence. Once we attain a state of security, we are equipped to comprehensively understand every facet of our being, encompassing not only the desirable and easily observable aspects. In this role, self-recognition is assured, and the unleashing of one's potential is inevitable. We are capable of recognizing our limitations, constraints, and imperfections; nonetheless, this consciousness does not hinder our ability to fully accept ourselves.

I typically advise my therapy clients that in order to genuinely improve their self-esteem, they must delve into the aspects of themselves that they have not yet been willing to recognize. Ultimately, the act of loving ourselves more or engaging in self-improvement entails primarily the practice of self-validation. Only after ceasing to engage in self-criticism are we able to ascertain a genuine sense of our own identity. What is the underlying cause for the natural increase in self-esteem when we cease to be excessively critical of ourselves? I consider it imperative for our happiness and state of well-being that self-acknowledgment encompasses significantly more than mere self-esteem, thereby serving as a fundamental aspect.

What is the underlying factor that leads to the resolution of our self-acceptance issues, or alternatively, contributes to our lack thereof?

Similar to self-esteem, during childhood, we are inclined to acknowledge ourselves only to the degree that we perceive acknowledgment from our parents. Research findings have indicated that prior to reaching the age of eight, it is a challenge to establish a distinctly defined sense of self that is independent from the influence of our caregivers. Hence, in the event that our family members were incapable or unwilling to convey the notion that we were fully competent and satisfactory, regardless of our challenging, occasionally wayward behavior, we were prepared to perceive ourselves as uncertain. The degree of respect we received from our elders may be contingent upon our behavior, and unfortunately, it came to our attention that a significant portion of our actions were deemed unsatisfactory by them. Hence, by acknowledging these reprehensible behaviors within ourselves, we inevitably came to regard ourselves as lacking in various aspects.

Furthermore, unfriendly affectionate assessment can, and every now and again do, go a long way past objecting bad practices. As an example, guardians may express the overall notion that we possess self-centered tendencies - or lack sufficient beauty, intelligence, goodness, or amiability... Etc. Due to the consensus among a majority of mental health professionals, it is widely recognized that we tend to perceive ourselves as inherently unworthy, which can be seen as a subtle form of psychological abuse. Consequently, we learn to conscientiously acknowledge various facets of our self that have been adversely impacted, painfully concealing emotions of rejection stemming from excessively critical parents. This habit toward self-criticism is at the core of the more crucial part of the problems that, as grown-ups, we accidentally make for ourselves.

Given the nature of cognitive processes in the human mind, it is exceedingly difficult to fathom deviating from the influence of our initial parental upbringing. If our caregivers subjected us to detrimental methods of upbringing, as adults, we would seek diverse means to perpetuate that lingering anguish. In the event that we frequently encounter being ignored, criticized, blamed, reprimanded, or subjected to physical discipline, we will inevitably develop a means to cope with such personal indignation. Therefore, when we figuratively "criticize ourselves harshly," we are frequently following in our parents' footsteps. We were significantly reliant on them during our youth, and as a result, when we encountered even a small amount of their influence, we carefully examined their diverse perspectives regarding us. Consequently, we mostly felt compelled to regard their negative assessments as valid. This statement merely serves to indicate that they consistently belittle and demean us. Historically, it can be acknowledged that guardians have exhibited a prominent inclination to communicate their concerns regarding our actions rather than rewarding us for our progressively refined and adept social behaviors.

In developing a comprehensive understanding of our current self-perceptions, it becomes imperative to consider the disapproval and examination we may have received from family members, acquaintances, educators - and notably, our companions, who (dealing with their own uncertainties) could hardly resist ridiculing our vulnerabilities whenever inadvertently exposed. However, it is a reasonable expectation that almost all of us begin the journey of maturity with a certain predisposition towards pessimism. We display a conventional propensity to assign blame to ourselves or perceive ourselves as being somehow flawed. It appears as though each of us, to varying degrees, inadvertently contributes to the adverse consequences stemming from an ongoing "infection" of skepticism in oneself.

Accepting ourselves authentically (regardless of our shortcomings) would have been nearly ingrained in us if our parents had imparted a resoundingly affirming message about our worth—and furthermore, we were raised in a consistently nurturing atmosphere. Contrary to that assertion, in fact, it is necessary for us to focus on the process of obtaining certification, in order to substantiate our essential competence. Furthermore, I am simply suggesting that our sole focus on self-validation is not necessarily synonymous with effectively addressing our inner conflicts; rather, it is about overcoming our inclination to consistently pass harsh judgments on ourselves. In order to attain perpetual depths of self-awareness and inner tranquility as a fundamental state of our existence, it is imperative that we initially fulfill societal expectations by wholly embracing and recognizing our own inherent qualities.

Engage in an activity that brings you joy

I was frustrated. On that particular day, I was burdened with an extensive list of tasks, primarily consisting of administrative duties related to the program I oversaw, which dealt with waste management and project coordination. I experienced profound distress and had a strong dislike for my current role, to the extent that it occasionally compelled me to seclude myself and weep.

It was midday that day, which provided some respite from the unpleasantness. Therefore, given the pleasant weather conditions of a summery day, I took the opportunity to visit the local park. Interestingly, historical records indicate that England once possessed such recreational spaces. However, in the present context, as I pen this initial edition, individuals are currently limited to venturing outdoors only once daily, ensuring a safe distance from others in light of the prevailing threat posed by the coronavirus.

On that particular day, I refrained from utilizing the slide and commencing the act of dispensing sustenance to the ducks using bread (although I inadvertently inverted the order of these activities in my previous statement, I considered retaining it as it elicited amusement).

I am undeniably taking a circuitous approach in recounting this anecdote... Nevertheless, I retrieved my notepad and commenced strategizing for my upcoming work of fantasy literature. Edge of Perfection. I became fully engrossed in the process of devising the narrative, allowing it to consume my thoughts and divert my attention away from my personal difficulties and the mundane affairs of the day, thus experiencing a rekindling of happiness within me. When lunch concluded, I experienced a tinge of melancholy as I reluctantly prepared to return, yet the overwhelming sensation that surged within me was truly unparalleled.

I experienced a sense of purpose, joy, and excitement.

When we are not engaged in activities that genuinely resonate with us, we fail to effectively communicate our true selves. Hence, it is for this reason that I am able to observe individuals experiencing profound unhappiness within their occupations. I have experienced considerable dissatisfaction in previous professional roles primarily due to a lack of personal affinity and a misalignment between my job responsibilities and my genuine passions.

I currently find myself in a favorable situation wherein I possess a clear understanding of my life goals. It solely hinges upon unwavering dedication to ongoing efforts, coupled with continuous enhancement of my marketing and sales acumen. I aspire to pursue a career as an author and public speaker. Additionally, I engage in coaching and mentoring individuals. I love it.

Each of these experiences fills me with exhilaration and a sense of being truly genuine.

Speaking is the aspect that profoundly alters my entire world. I am currently experiencing a sensation of goosebumps, however, when I am engaged in public speaking, nothing quite compares to the exhilaration that it brings. When I am articulating my insights on subjects that

I believe can be beneficial to others, I experience a sense of invulnerability. At present, I humbly acknowledge that I may not possess exemplary skills in public speaking; nevertheless, I possess a fervent passion for it and perpetually strive for self-improvement.

I kindly request and encourage you to discover and pursue your passion or calling. It may not be solely through verbal communication, but there exists a certain means. Possible alternative: "It encompasses a wide range of activities, such as dance, creative writing, visual arts, athletics, tennis, video game design, baking, and ballroom dancing." Do not allow yourself to experience any sense of shame regarding its nature. Furthermore, the individuals who criticize your pursuits are likely those who hesitate to venture beyond their customary routines or strive to fulfill their ambitions.

You may currently possess knowledge of it, or you may not possess such knowledge.

If you opt to do so, ensure that you dedicate time to this endeavor on a daily basis, as it will allow your authentic self to emerge and consequently enhance your sense of self-worth.

If you opt not to, that is perfectly acceptable. Do not burden yourself excessively due to your lack of knowledge, but do ensure that you set aside time to discover that genuine pursuit. Reflecting upon the activities that brought you joy during your childhood is consistently beneficial.

Currently, I am composing this piece effortlessly, and I thoroughly enjoy the process. I highly recommend the book 'Super Attractor' by Gabby Bernstein, which offers valuable insights on cultivating a positive emotional state. This study examines the significance of prioritizing emotional well-being over the desired outcome, as experiencing positive emotions facilitates smoother progress and ultimately better results. Think about it? Do you derive pleasure from engaging in activities that align with your passions?

What are the consequences of failing to achieve the desired outcomes when implementing a course of action? You regain a sense of pleasure in immersing yourself in the activity you are passionate about and living in the present moment. Seeking counsel from a mentor or coach, you then embark on a renewed pursuit.

Action:

If one is aware of their genuine passion, it is advisable to allocate a minimum of twenty minutes per day (ideally more, if possible) in their schedule for engaging in said passion.

If you are uncertain about it, I recommend allocating a specific duration for exploring and determining your genuine passion. I will provide a set of questions below in order to assist you.

Questions to get you started on doing what you love:

What activities did you particularly enjoy during your childhood?

If you were faced with a six-month time frame remaining, what actions would you undertake? (I beg your pardon for the solemnity, but it proved beneficial to me.)

May I inquire about your areas of proficiency or personal interests? (You are also permitted to derive pleasure from activities in which you lack proficiency!)

- What is it about that activity that captures your full attention, causing you to disregard everything else? (Kindly refrain from providing responses involving the consumption of alcohol or drugs.)

If you were bestowed with a remarkable talent, what particular skill or ability would you choose to develop?

The Efficacy Of Optimistic Mindset

There is no more effective means by which one may enhance their self-esteem expeditiously than the approach we are presently underscoring. Step 3 involves harnessing the potential of optimistic thought patterns. Positive thinking encompasses the emotional and cognitive disposition and capacity to dwell upon the favorable aspects and anticipate their manifestation in one's life. This anticipatory notion possesses the ability to elevate one's sense of self-worth from a state of low self-esteem to a state of self-acceptance.

The efficacy of maintaining an optimistic mindset leads individuals towards optimal physical well-being, contentment, and accomplishment in various domains of life. The efficacy of optimistic thought processes engenders a profound internal conviction, enabling individuals to surmount adversities, setbacks, and impediments.

In order for you to attain success and enhance your self-esteem, the adoption of positive thinking needs to transcend mere verbal expression and become an ingrained aspect of your everyday existence. It is imperative for it to transform into a state of existence as opposed to merely a state of cognition. Let us examine the components encompassed within this approach.

- The Influence of Cognitive Processes and Concepts

Many individuals frequently struggle to place faith in the ability of thoughts and ideas to materialize in the tangible realm. The notion that one can manifest their thoughts into reality is, to a certain extent, "inconceivable." Nevertheless, the veracity of the statement is unequivocal, and it requires only a handful of instances to foster conviction in its validity.

Let us consider a scenario wherein two individuals are striving towards a common objective. One individual holds the belief that he or she will attain it, while the other individual maintains the conviction that he or she will not acquire it. What do think happens? What if two opposing teams strive for the same triumph? The entire team collectively holds the belief that they will emerge victorious. The opposing team comprises individuals who hold divergent perspectives on their chances of success: some exude confidence in winning, while others express doubt, and a few individuals harbor apprehension despite their awareness of their inherent capabilities to emerge victorious. What are your thoughts on the potential outcome? The true query resides in what insights does our collective experience offer regarding the course of events?

In the initial scenario, individuals who possess unwavering belief in their ability to achieve a goal are likely to realize it, whereas those lacking self-confidence will invariably fall short of accomplishing said goal. The team that collectively holds the belief that they will emerge victorious shall indeed emerge victorious. Another lesson that can be gleaned from the team is their collective conviction and expectation of victory, which they ultimately achieve. Positive thinking is contagious. Additionally, one can derive valuable insight from the team that did not emerge victorious, which is that pessimistic thoughts can be just as infectious.

The individuals in our vicinity undeniably exert a profound influence on us, be it overt, subconscious, or innate in nature. The non-verbal cues, verbal communication, emotional state, and cognitive processes of others greatly influence our responses at an intuitive and unconscious level.

Pessimistic thoughts give rise to adverse emotions and conduct. Analogously, the cultivation of optimistic thoughts engenders positive emotions and conduct. As a result, individuals are inclined to seek our company, extend their assistance, and positive outcomes manifest in our lives. It is crucial that we remain cognizant of any detrimental emotions that arise within our thoughts and promptly address them.

Learn how to effectively replace your negative thoughts with positive ones through self-guided instruction. Make it a habit to engage in this practice whenever a negative thought arises. Be persistent. It will eventually work. You are cultivating your mind, as has been the customary practice among individuals throughout history. You are actively or passively cultivating a mindset of positive thinking. Let us now explore alternative methodologies for cultivating mental acuity.

- Confirmations - Louise Hay

Louise Hay, an American individual, received a diagnosis of a terminal illness and exhibited strong resolve to alter her circumstances. Medical professionals asserted that there were no viable interventions, yet Louise maintained unwavering conviction in the power of psychological fortitude. To put it differently, the power of thoughts lies in their ability to shape the tangible aspects of reality. Louise successfully applied her personal convictions and skillfully crafted a methodology centered around affirmations, initially for the preservation of her own life, subsequently extending her assistance to aid others in safeguarding and enhancing their own lives.

The utilization of affirmations is the pivotal factor in Hay's ability to persevere and in augmenting one's self-confidence. Her inaugural literary achievement is the timeless masterpiece entitled You Can Heal Your Life. She is a trailblazer in the realm of assertions and a testament to the transformative power of optimistic mindset in shaping both physical and emotional actuality. Utilizing affirmations can enhance your self-esteem at this present moment. Commitment and perseverance from your end are crucial ingredients for success.

Affirmations encompass constructive thoughts that are vocalized regularly to oneself. Affirmations comprise statements akin to the following renowned affirmation by Louise Hay: "With each passing day, I am steadily improving and progressing in various domains". By diligently engaging with her literature and utilizing her audio materials, one can swiftly enhance their self-esteem.

- An educational program centered around the principles of miracles

A Course in Miracles is furthermore a literary work authored and revised by Helen Schuman, and transcribed and revised by William Thetford, whose fundamental proposition bears notable resemblance to the concepts previously deliberated upon in this chapter. The focal point lies in the "Workbook" that provides a daily lesson for each day throughout the year. The objective of these lessons is to facilitate a transition in your mindset from "judgment motivated by fear" to "forgiveness driven by love".

Furthermore, the authors contend that the alteration in cognitive processes leads to corresponding modifications in behavior and emotional experiences, not only affecting the individual who undergoes the change, but also influencing those in their immediate environment. The teachings emphasize the interconnectedness among all beings, as well as the importance of self-forgiveness and forgiveness toward others. The workbook encourages you to have unwavering trust in its guidance, with the expectation that through consistent practice, you will gradually manifest your desired reality and cultivate the qualities that define the person you aspire to become.

You may perceive A Course in Miracles as overly challenging. This concept revolves around the perception of life and oneself, envisioning them according to personal desires and subsequently manifesting them through the power of thought, regardless of one's belief in their achievability. If you presently observe and depict your diminished self-worth, your desolation, and your resentment in an outward manner, you shall witness yourself and perceive the world through that lens. Conversely, should you acquire the ability to emanate love and exhibit forgiveness towards others, you will observe both yourself and the world through that lens, resulting in an elevation of your self-esteem. Above all, it is imperative to demonstrate self-forgiveness.

- Synopsis and Course of Action

In the preceding chapter, we have examined the notion of materializing one's mental constructs into the external realm, effectively giving form to our thoughts through the power of conscious deliberation. Individuals possess the ability to shape their own levels of self-esteem through their thoughts, and they can acquire the skill of cultivating positive thinking. Please find below a set of strategies to assist you in accomplishing this objective.

- Allocate sufficient time for perusing literature on the concepts of optimistic thinking, affirmations, and materializing your desires by harnessing the power of your thoughts. There is a wealth of digital articles and e-books accessible through online platforms, such as Kindle, in addition to the resources found in the library.

- Cultivate the habit of envisioning exclusively favorable circumstances and emotions.
- Engage in the exercise of mentally picturing solely constructive situations and sensations.
- Train yourself to imagine exclusively optimistic scenarios and emotions.
- Foster the practice of visualizing nothing but positive circumstances and feelings.
- Dedicate yourself to the task of mentally constructing only favorable situations and emotions.
- Employ solely optimistic language when communicating with oneself or interacting with others.
- Compose several constructive affirmations and engage in daily vocal repetition, reciting them a minimum of ten consecutive times.

An individual is merely a manifestation of his or her thoughts - what one ponders, one eventually becomes.
Mahatma Gandhi

4. Engage in frequent expressions of happiness, such as smiling and laughing.

Expressing joy and amusement stands in direct contrast to experiencing sorrow or negativity. By assimilating this new practice into your daily routine, you will inevitably experience a heightened sense of well-being and optimism.

There exists a profound interrelation between the body and mind. Our thoughts and feelings are influenced by the manner in which we utilize our physical body.

A genuine or even artificially induced smile has the immediate effect of eliciting feelings of happiness within oneself. This is an excellent method to enhance your emotional well-being and promote a sense of positivity among those in your vicinity.

Try this exercise. Assume a position in front of your reflective surface, direct your gaze upon your own countenance, and deliberately manifest a smile or display amusement.

One can either feign a smile or reminisce about a person, child, pet, situation, or any other source of happiness that elicits a smile. Both of them will perform exceedingly well.

It swiftly inundates you with a profound sense of positivity. Keep it up, and you won't be able to stop smiling.

Please proceed to attempt it immediately.

During the execution of this exercise, I consistently find myself succumbing to laughter. I am also of a positive mindset...You have the ability to achieve the same result!

According to scientific research, laughter and smiling have been found to possess therapeutic properties that can alleviate ailments and feelings of depression.

It is advisable to cultivate a frequent display of smiles and laughter. It will enhance the positivity in your daily life and radiate to those in your immediate vicinity. It is advantageous for all parties involved.

5. Exercise

A sound physical state is a prerequisite for maintaining a sound mental state.

Physical activity not only induces alterations in your physique, but it also induces modifications in your emotional state.

Physical activity enhances blood circulation throughout the entirety of the body, including the cerebral region. It results in an augmented provision of oxygen and nutrients, which function as sustenance for the brain. Additionally, an abundance of hormones is secreted, contributing to enhanced cognitive functions within the brain. A few examples of these hormones include:

Endorphins: They serve to decrease stress levels and promote relaxation. As a consequence, they contribute to alleviating anxiety and depression. In addition, they diminish discomfort and alleviate pain while amplifying delight and bolstering self-confidence.

Serotonin performs the function of regulating appetite, enhancing sleep quality, and exerting an impact on emotional state. All of these factors are interconnected and mutually contribute to enhancing our sense of happiness, tranquility, and optimism.

Dopamine serves as a messenger that activates regions in our brain associated with the experience of reward and pleasure. It governs our levels of motivation and consequently dictates the extent to which we undertake proactive measures towards achieving our objectives.

Testosterone plays a significant role in the physiological functioning of individuals, regardless of their gender. It governs your metabolic processes, muscle development, and sexual libido. Insufficient levels of testosterone have the potential to lead to depression and obesity.

The implication is that, by continually engaging in a state of leisure on your couch throughout the day, you fail to provide your brain with the opportunity to function to its maximum capacity.

I earnestly recommend allocating at least 30 minutes each day towards engaging in physical exercise. This can encompass various activities such as walking, jogging, cycling, weightlifting, cardio workouts, yoga, or tai-chi. Feel free to choose whichever activity aligns with your preferences. It is advisable to consult with your physician prior to commencing.

Furthermore, aside from the aforementioned morning exercise routine, it is advisable to rise from your seat at half-hour intervals to engage in leg-stretching activities. Engage in a brief perambulation within the premises of the office. Please proceed to the water cooler, consume a small amount of liquid, and return promptly. Please consider rising and engaging in some physical activity.

Attempt to engage in both of these activities for a duration of 10 consecutive days. You will undoubtedly observe a significant enhancement in both your positivity and energy levels. Engaging in physical activity rejuvenates the mind and body, instilling vitality into your daily routine.

6. Meditation

Throughout our day, our mental faculties are fully engaged in continuous contemplation. It is impossible to entirely cease cognitive processes. No matter how diligently one endeavors to eradicate every thought, it shall prove futile. Within the context of Buddhist culture, this phenomenon is referred to as the mental state known as the "monkey brain." In this state, our thoughts and focus exhibit an unrestrained tendency to wander in a sporadic and unpredictable manner.

In order to achieve tranquility and contentment, it is imperative that we exercise dominion over our thoughts and emotions. The ultimate form of liberty lies in emancipation from cognitive processes.

Imagine that you are engaged in a harmonious and lighthearted interaction with your significant other within the confines of your own dwelling, while concurrently experiencing mental preoccupation with the task of finalizing a project report prior to the midday meal on the following day. What level of effectiveness would that conversation possess?

Meditation cultivates mindfulness, enabling individuals to wholly engage with the present moment, consequently fostering a greater sense of happiness and equipping them with the capacity to effectively navigate adversities. Research indicates that mindfulness practice not only serves as a efficacious therapeutic intervention for various prevalent medical conditions, but also exhibits the potential to enhance individual well-being, foster empathy, and cultivate compassion towards others.

Individuals who engage in the practice of meditation also encounter reduced levels of anxiety, anger, and mental stress, in addition to a heightened state of presence, positivity, and serenity. Meditation can serve as a beneficial endeavor for individuals with a history of trauma.

The meditation technique that requires minimal effort:

Please configure an alarm for a duration of 10 to 15 minutes.

Please take a seat on the chair, ensuring that your back is both relaxed and properly aligned in an upright position.

Please close your eyes and carefully observe the flow of your breath entering and exiting your body. Observe every aspect of it—from the moment it enters your nasal passages to the point it reaches your diaphragm. The undulating motion of your abdomen, ascending and descending, and so forth.

In due course, your mind will commence contemplation on a particular matter. You are prone to becoming deeply absorbed in contemplation. One's attention shifts away from their breath and fixates upon the thought at hand. It is permissible. Whenever you find yourself fixating on your thoughts rather than maintaining an awareness of your breath, kindly and composedly redirect your attention to your breath.

It is inevitable that you will once again become disoriented within your thoughts and consequently lose your concentration. Once more, redirect your attention tranquilly towards your breath.

Continue performing this action until the sounding of your alarm.

This straightforward practice is highly effective in significantly enhancing the overall state of your mind, encompassing elements such as tranquility, optimism, mental clarity, attentiveness, determination, and concentration. The efficacy of this approach has been substantiated through extensive research conducted internationally.

Try it yourself.

7. Help Other People

Assisting others brings me greater satisfaction than solely fulfilling my personal requirements.

If your intention is to assist others, undertake this endeavor with sincerity. Do not engage in such actions solely for the sake of doing so. Demonstrate empathy and kindness. Make an effort to empathize with their perspective and gain a broader understanding of their

experiences. Subsequently, exert all possible efforts to assist them.
It will provide you with an abundance of joy far beyond your wildest dreams.

Acknowledging One's Own Emotions as a Platform for Development

The ability to acknowledge your own emotions serves as the foundation for subsequently acknowledging the emotions of others. Hence, empathy and emotional intelligence are comprised of multiple emotional aptitudes rather than just one. This should prompt individuals to comprehend that achieving effective emotional intelligence necessitates the integration of multiple emotional stages in order to foster interconnectedness. If your sole focus is on acknowledging your own emotions, then your comprehension of others' emotions is lacking, resulting in a deficiency of emotional intelligence in your conduct.

Consequently, subsequent to acknowledging one's own emotions, it is imperative to evaluate and comprehend the emotions of others. The driver who abruptly changes lanes in front of another vehicle might acknowledge their emotional state, such as experiencing frustration due to being behind schedule, intense anger resulting from a prior incident of being cut off and the desire for retaliation, or a sense of euphoria caused by the unexpected discovery of a parking space when not anticipating one. They may acknowledge these emotions, but they thereafter need to distance themselves and evaluate the emotions of the other individuals involved in order to exhibit empathy and emotional intelligence.

The recommended course of action for an individual facing this circumstance would be to inquire: "

Are there any additional individuals involved in this matter whom I should take into consideration?

(2) What are the sentiments and aspirations held by the other individuals involved?

(3) How does the emotional and desire-related states of others relate to me and

the forthcoming actions that I am about to undertake?

(4) How can I demonstrate empathy and genuine concern for the emotions of others through my actions?

While there are individuals who contend that it is foolish and inconsequential to consistently contemplate the sentiments and aspirations of others, if one subscribes to the concept of emotional intelligence and acknowledges its potency, as well as recognizing empathy as a skill that merits cultivation, it becomes imperative to consciously engage in the process of pondering and comprehending the emotions of fellow individuals. Had the character in the film followed these steps, she would have discerned that another individual had been awaiting that parking spot and could have been undergoing their own sentiments of sorrow, wrath, and vexation. Upon engaging in this particular line of thinking, it would be within their reasonable expectations to procure an alternative parking area as a demonstration of sympathy or even empathy towards the circumstances encountered by the other party.

Hence, acknowledging one's own emotions serves as an initial step in cultivating empathetic conduct towards others. Certainly, the mere acknowledgment of individual emotions does not inherently result in the cultivation of sympathy, empathy, or emotional intelligence within ourselves. If individuals of both genders exclusively prioritize the acknowledgement of their own emotions, while remaining indifferent to the emotions experienced by others, they are, in essence, displaying narcissistic tendencies that stand in direct opposition to the empathetic values this book endeavors to promote.

It can be somewhat disconcerting that narcissism and empathy are intricately connected, yet terrestrial existence abounds with such dichotomies. Thriving harmoniously on this planet necessitates comprehending the equilibrium inherent in the inherent state of affairs in Earth's biosphere. As a sentient species, we are inherently designed to coexist with individuals from our own species as well as with individuals belonging to other species, maintaining a state of harmony and equilibrium. The exclusive prioritization of our own emotions and desires leads to a state of imbalance, consequently affecting the harmony of our surroundings. The mere manifestation of egocentric behavior by an individual can precipitate a ripple effect, causing others to follow suit, thereby resulting in a disruption of the equilibrium within a social collective, in conflict with the inherent laws of nature.

www.ingramcontent.com/pod-product-compliance
Lightning Source LLC
Chambersburg PA
CBHW050243120526
44590CB00016B/2199